1st page torn -12/11 YH

DATE DUE		
~~DEC 16 2011~~		
~~MAR 3 1 2012~~	~~MAR 2 8 2013~~	

ROSA PARKS

AND THE Montgomery Bus Boycott

by Connie Colwell Miller
illustrated by Dan Kalal

Consultant:
Charles P. Henry, PhD
Professor, African American Studies
University of California, Berkeley

Capstone
press

Mankato, Minnesota

Graphic Library is published by Capstone Press,
151 Good Counsel Drive, P.O. Box 669, Mankato, Minnesota 56002.
www.capstonepress.com

Printed in the United States of America

1 2 3 4 5 6 11 10 09 08 07 06

Library of Congress Cataloging-in-Publication Data
Miller, Connie Colwell, 1976–
Rosa Parks and the Montgomery bus boycott / by Connie Colwell Miller.
p. cm.—(Graphic library. Graphic biographies)
Includes bibliographical references and index.
ISBN-13: 978-0-7368-6495-4 (hardcover)
ISBN-10: 0-7368-6495-4 (hardcover)
ISBN-13: 978-0-7368-9658-0 (softcover pbk.)
ISBN-10: 0-7368-9658-9 (softcover pbk.)
1. Parks, Rosa, 1913–2005—Juvenile literature. 2. African American women—Alabama—Montgomery—Biography—Juvenile literature. 3. African Americans—Alabama—Montgomery—Biography—Juvenile literature. 4. Civil rights workers—Alabama—Montgomery—Biography—Juvenile literature. 5. African Americans—Civil rights—Alabama—Montgomery—History—20th century—Juvenile literature. 6. Segregation in transportation—Alabama—Montgomery—History—20th century—Juvenile literature. 7. Montgomery (Ala.)—Race relations—Juvenile literature. 8. Montgomery (Ala.)—Biography—Juvenile literature. I. Title. II. Series.
F334.M753M55 2007
323.092—dc22 2006004841

Summary: In graphic novel format, tells the story of Rosa Park's arrest for not giving up her bus seat on December 1, 1955, and the boycott it sparked.

Designer
Alison Thiele

Colorist
Michael Kelleher

Editor
Erika L. Shores

Editor's note: Direct quotations from primary sources are indicated by a yellow background.

Direct quotations appear on the following pages:
Pages 6, 7, 8, 9, 11 (top), 25, 26, from Douglas Brinkley's interviews with Rosa Parks as quoted in *Rosa Parks* by Douglas Brinkley (New York: Viking, 2000).
Page 11 (bottom), from *The Montgomery Bus Boycott and the Women Who Started It: The Memoir of Jo Ann Gibson Robinson* by Jo Ann Gibson Robinson (Knoxville: University of Tennessee Press, 1987).
Page 21, from *The Autobiography of Martin Luther King Jr.* edited by Clayborne Carson (New York: Intellectual Properties Management in association with Warner Books, 1998).

TABLE OF CONTENTS

Chapter 1
Rosa Takes a Stand

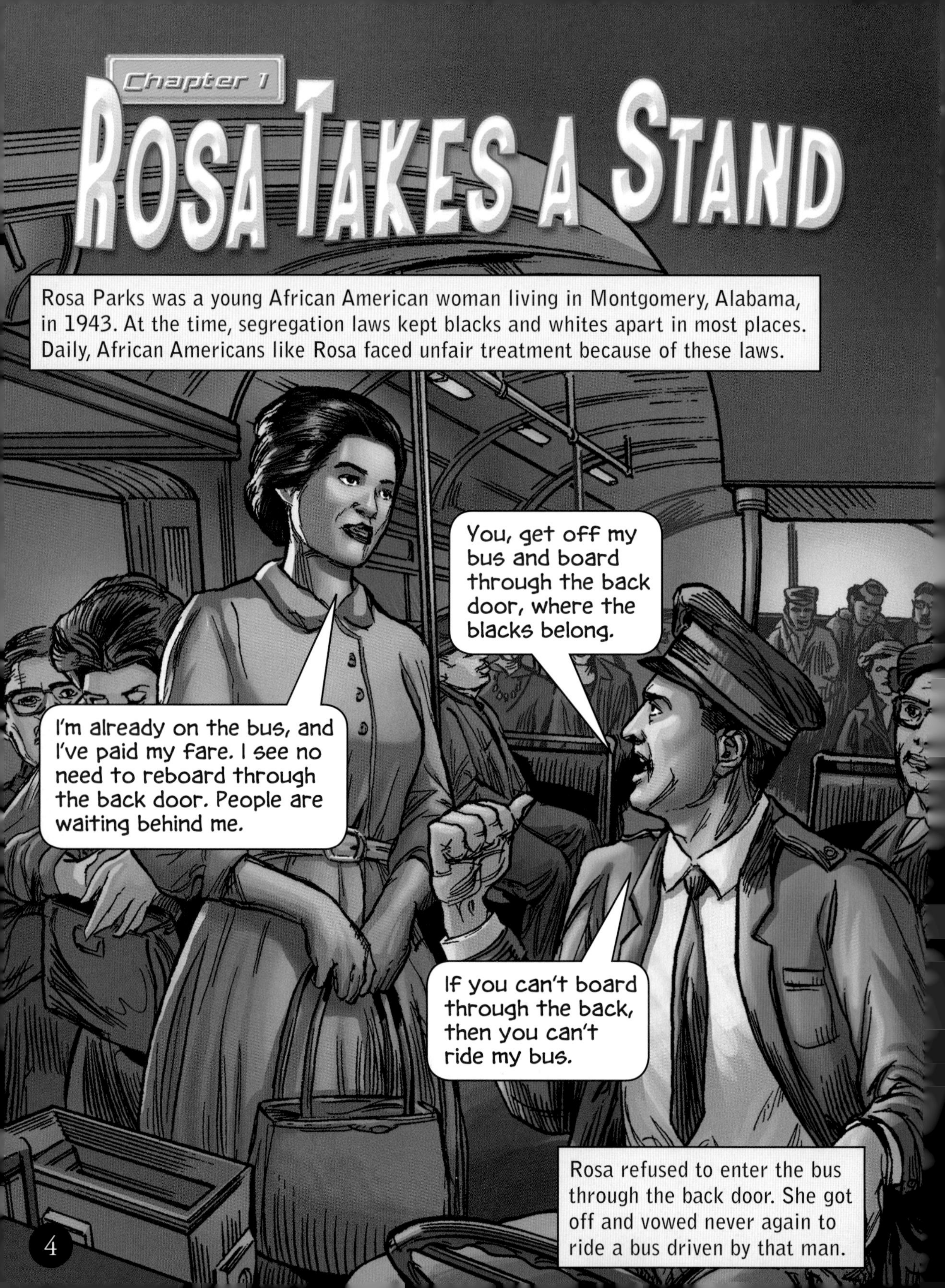

Rosa Parks was a young African American woman living in Montgomery, Alabama, in 1943. At the time, segregation laws kept blacks and whites apart in most places. Daily, African Americans like Rosa faced unfair treatment because of these laws.
You, get off my bus and board through the back door, where the blacks belong.
I'm already on the bus, and I've paid my fare. I see no need to reboard through the back door. People are waiting behind me.
If you can't board through the back, then you can't ride my bus.
Rosa refused to enter the bus through the back door. She got off and vowed never again to ride a bus driven by that man.

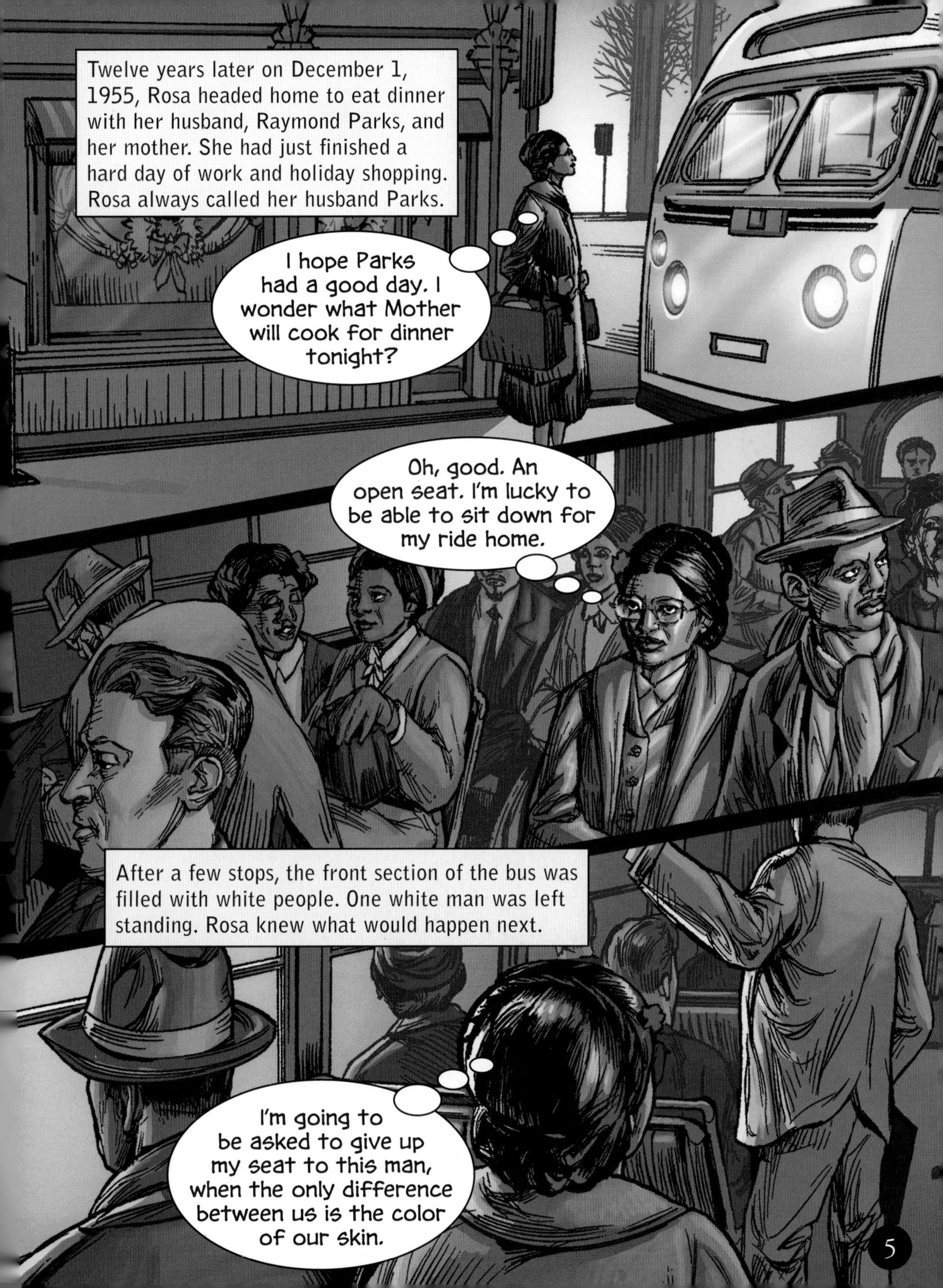
Twelve years later on December 1, 1955, Rosa headed home to eat dinner with her husband, Raymond Parks, and her mother. She had just finished a hard day of work and holiday shopping. Rosa always called her husband Parks.
I hope Parks had a good day. I wonder what Mother will cook for dinner tonight?
Oh, good. An open seat. I'm lucky to be able to sit down for my ride home.
After a few stops, the front section of the bus was filled with white people. One white man was left standing. Rosa knew what would happen next.
I'm going to be asked to give up my seat to this man, when the only difference between us is the color of our skin.

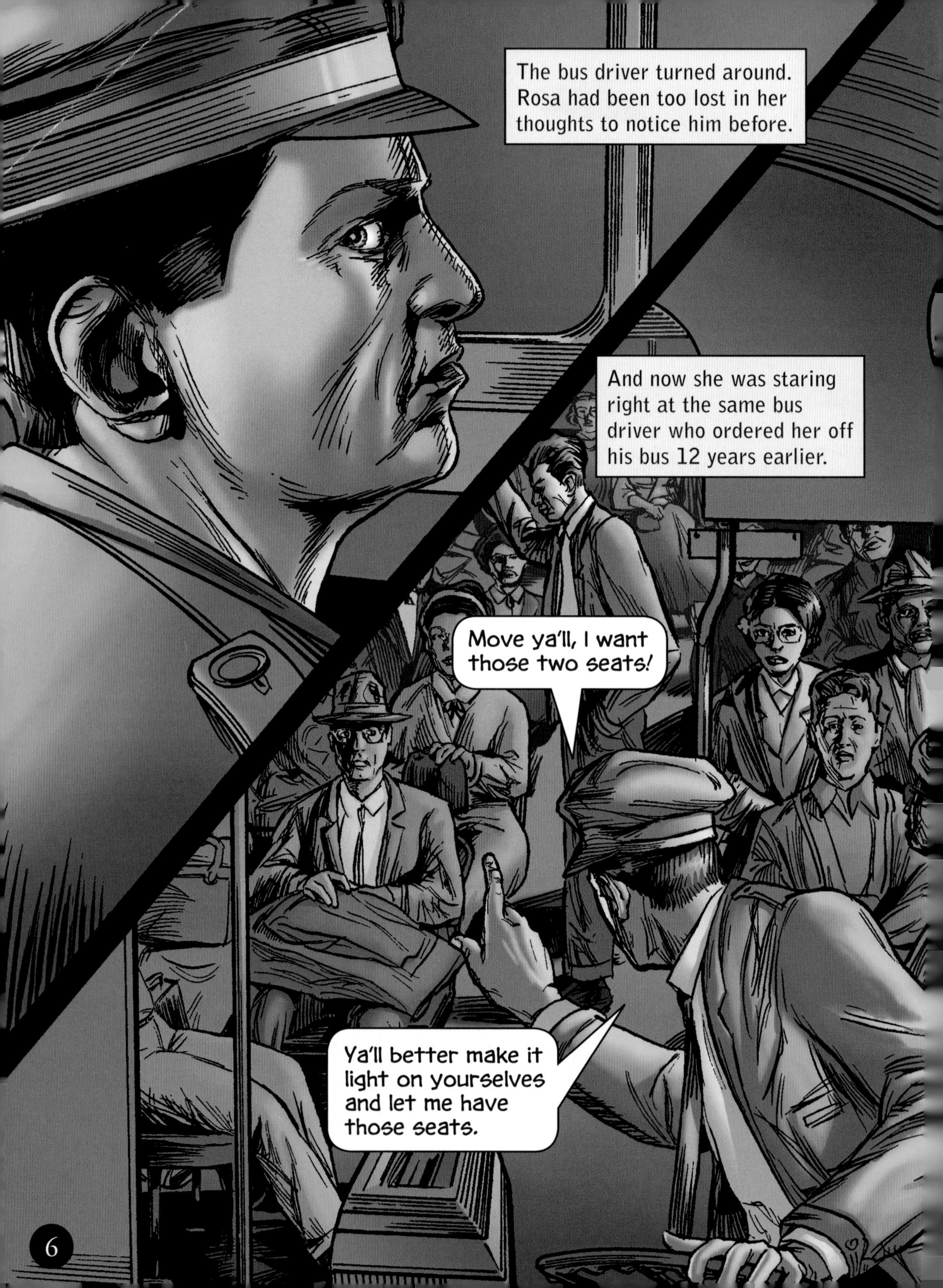
The bus driver turned around. Rosa had been too lost in her thoughts to notice him before.
And now she was staring right at the same bus driver who ordered her off his bus 12 years earlier.
Move ya'll, I want those two seats!
Ya'll better make it light on yourselves and let me have those seats.

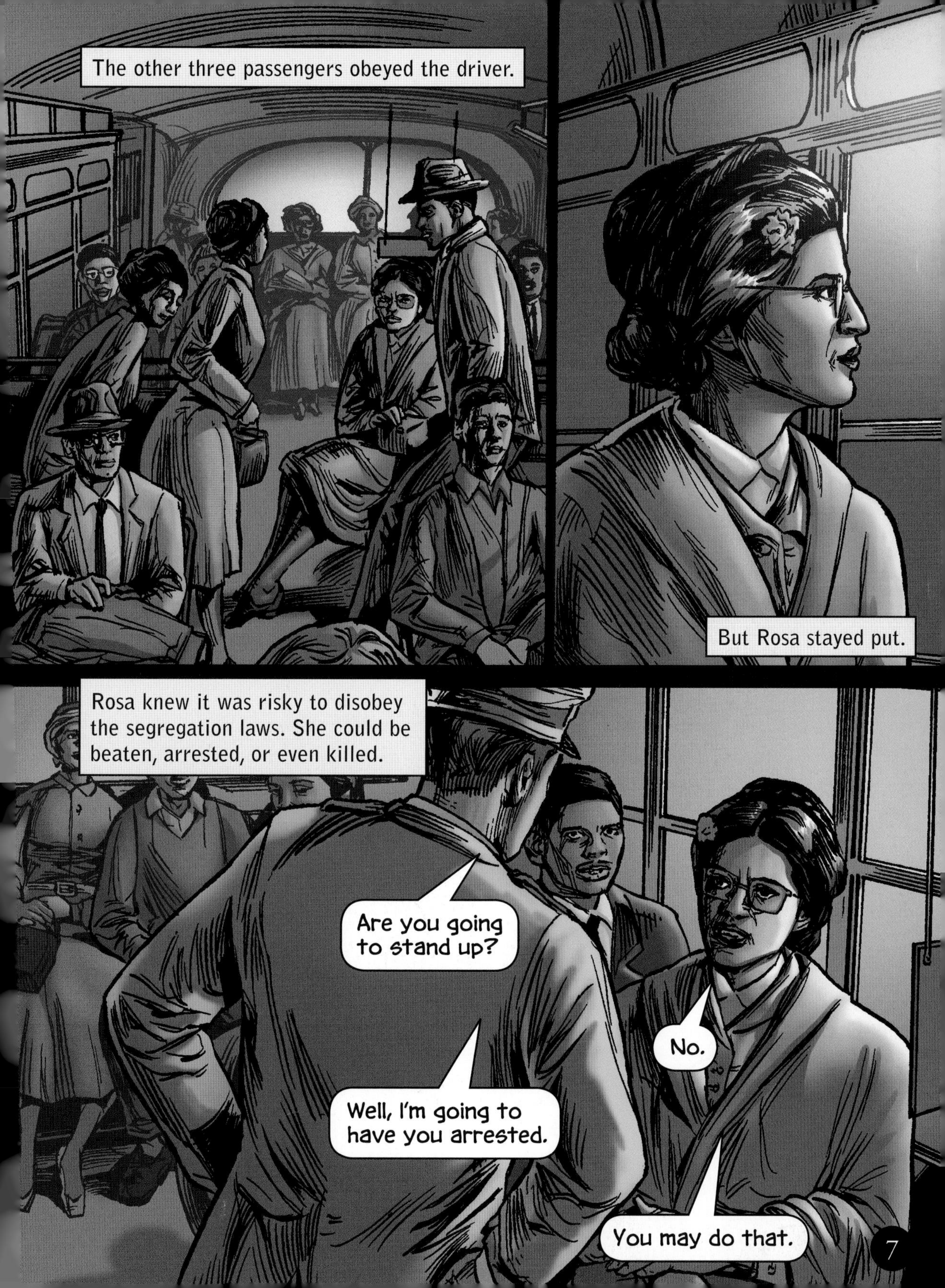
The other three passengers obeyed the driver.
But Rosa stayed put.
Rosa knew it was risky to disobey the segregation laws. She could be beaten, arrested, or even killed.
Are you going to stand up?
No.
Well, I'm going to have you arrested.
You may do that.

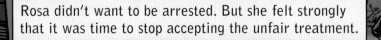

Rosa didn't want to be arrested. But she felt strongly that it was time to stop accepting the unfair treatment.

I'm a good person, and I always do what's right. It's not me who's wrong; it's this law.

You look like a nice lady. Why did you refuse to stand?

Why do you all push us around?

I don't know, but the law is the law, and you're under arrest.

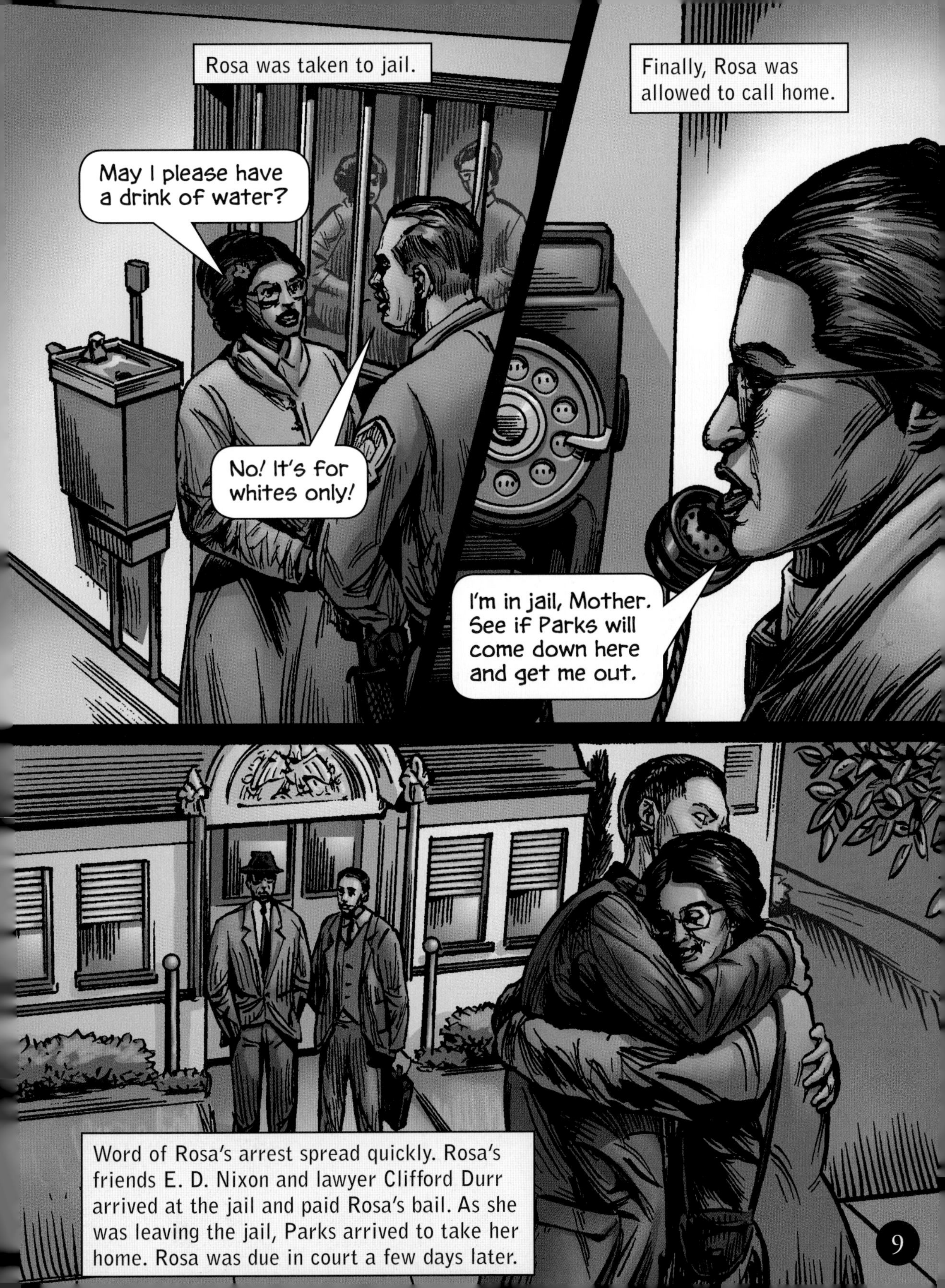
Rosa was taken to jail.
May I please have a drink of water?
No! It's for whites only!
Finally, Rosa was allowed to call home.
I'm in jail, Mother. See if Parks will come down here and get me out.
Word of Rosa's arrest spread quickly. Rosa's friends E. D. Nixon and lawyer Clifford Durr arrived at the jail and paid Rosa's bail. As she was leaving the jail, Parks arrived to take her home. Rosa was due in court a few days later.

Chapter 2

The Bus Boycott

For more than 12 years, Rosa had been a member of the NAACP. This organization wanted fair treatment for African Americans. Nixon was a former president of Montgomery's NAACP. As a secretary for the NAACP, Rosa had worked with Nixon. The night of Rosa's arrest, Nixon met with her and her family.

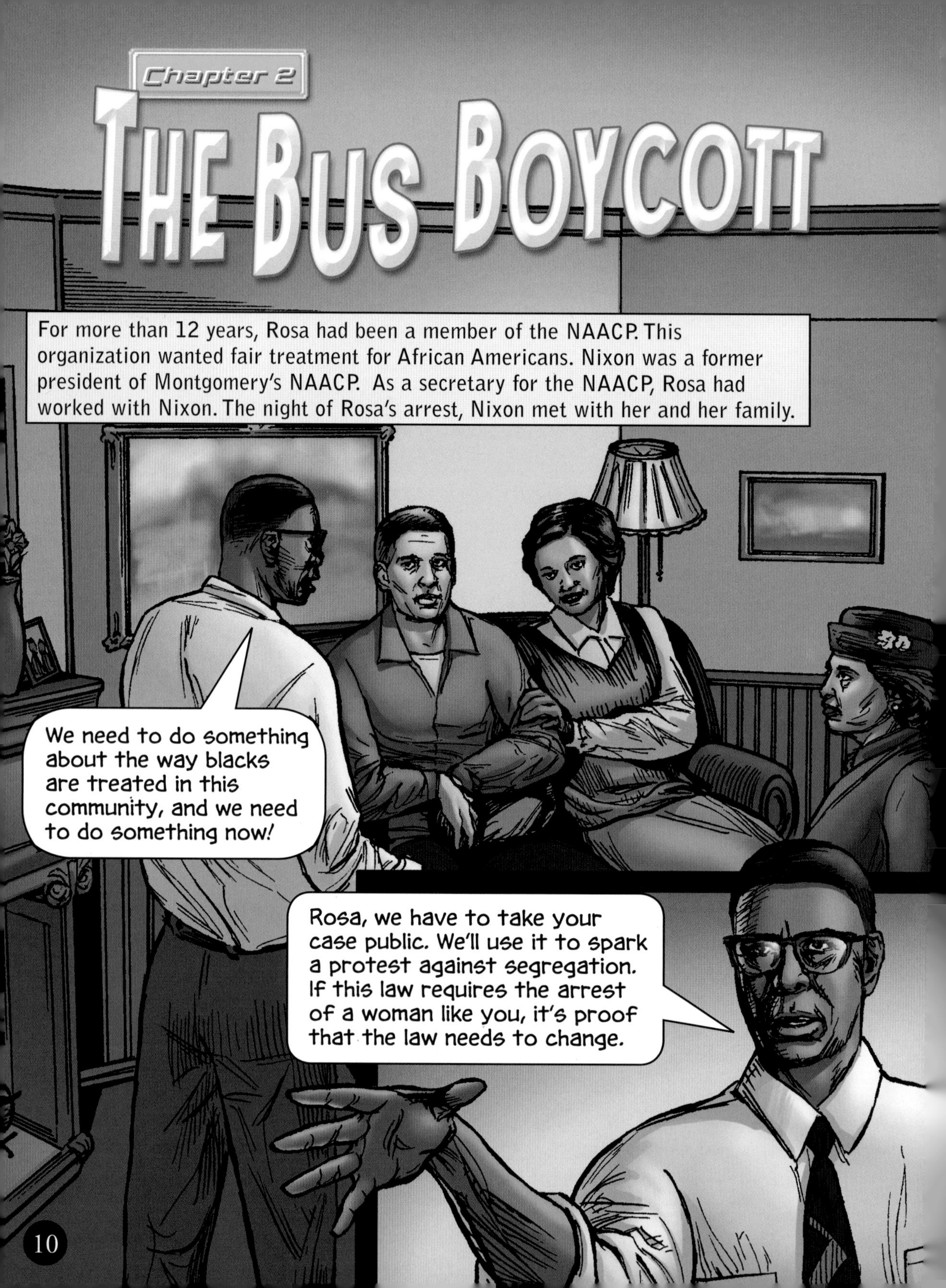
We need to do something about the way blacks are treated in this community, and we need to do something now!
Rosa, we have to take your case public. We'll use it to spark a protest against segregation. If this law requires the arrest of a woman like you, it's proof that the law needs to change.

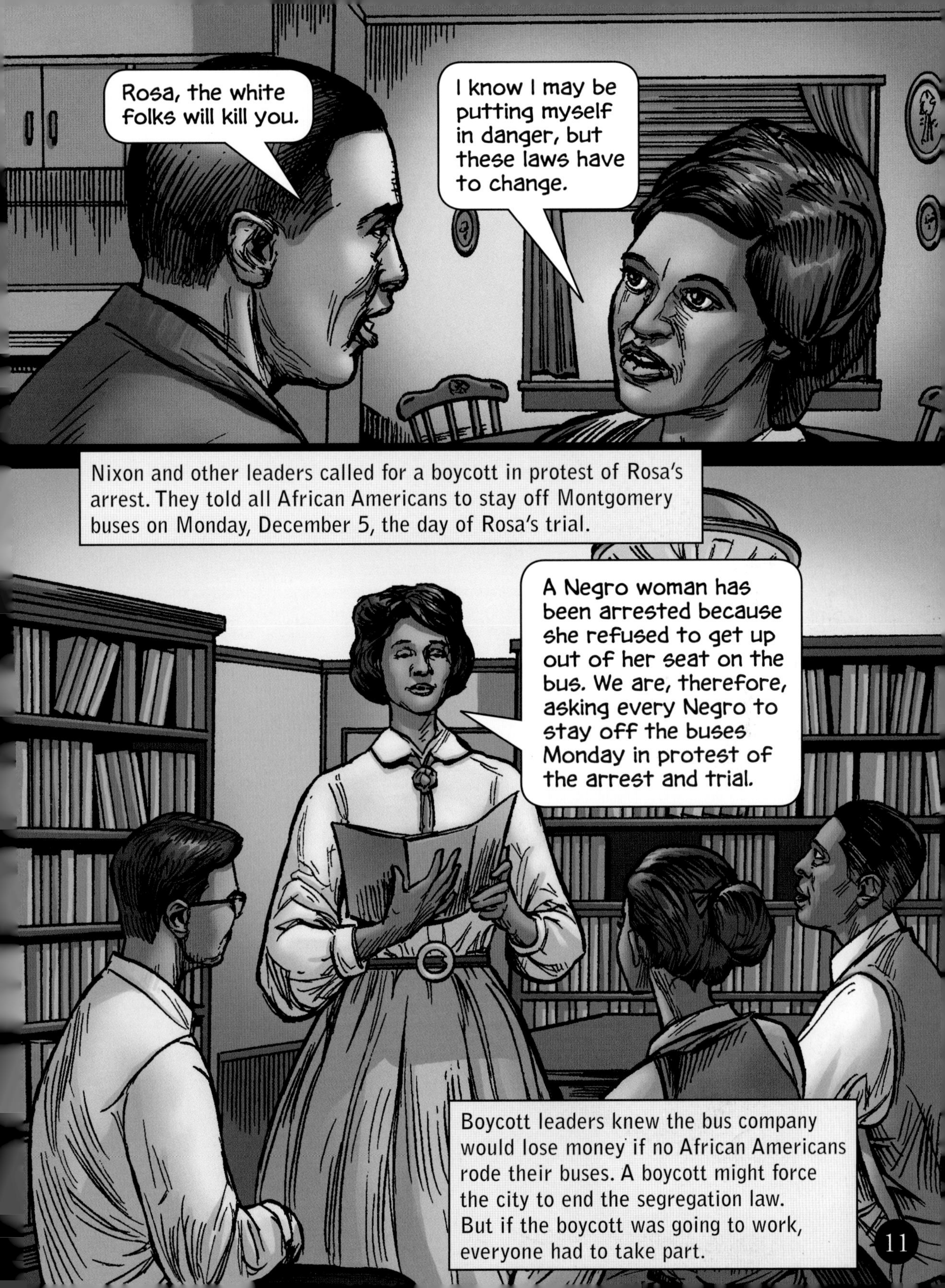
Rosa, the white folks will kill you.
I know I may be putting myself in danger, but these laws have to change.
Nixon and other leaders called for a boycott in protest of Rosa's arrest. They told all African Americans to stay off Montgomery buses on Monday, December 5, the day of Rosa's trial.
A Negro woman has been arrested because she refused to get up out of her seat on the bus. We are, therefore, asking every Negro to stay off the buses Monday in protest of the arrest and trial.
Boycott leaders knew the bus company would lose money if no African Americans rode their buses. A boycott might force the city to end the segregation law. But if the boycott was going to work, everyone had to take part.

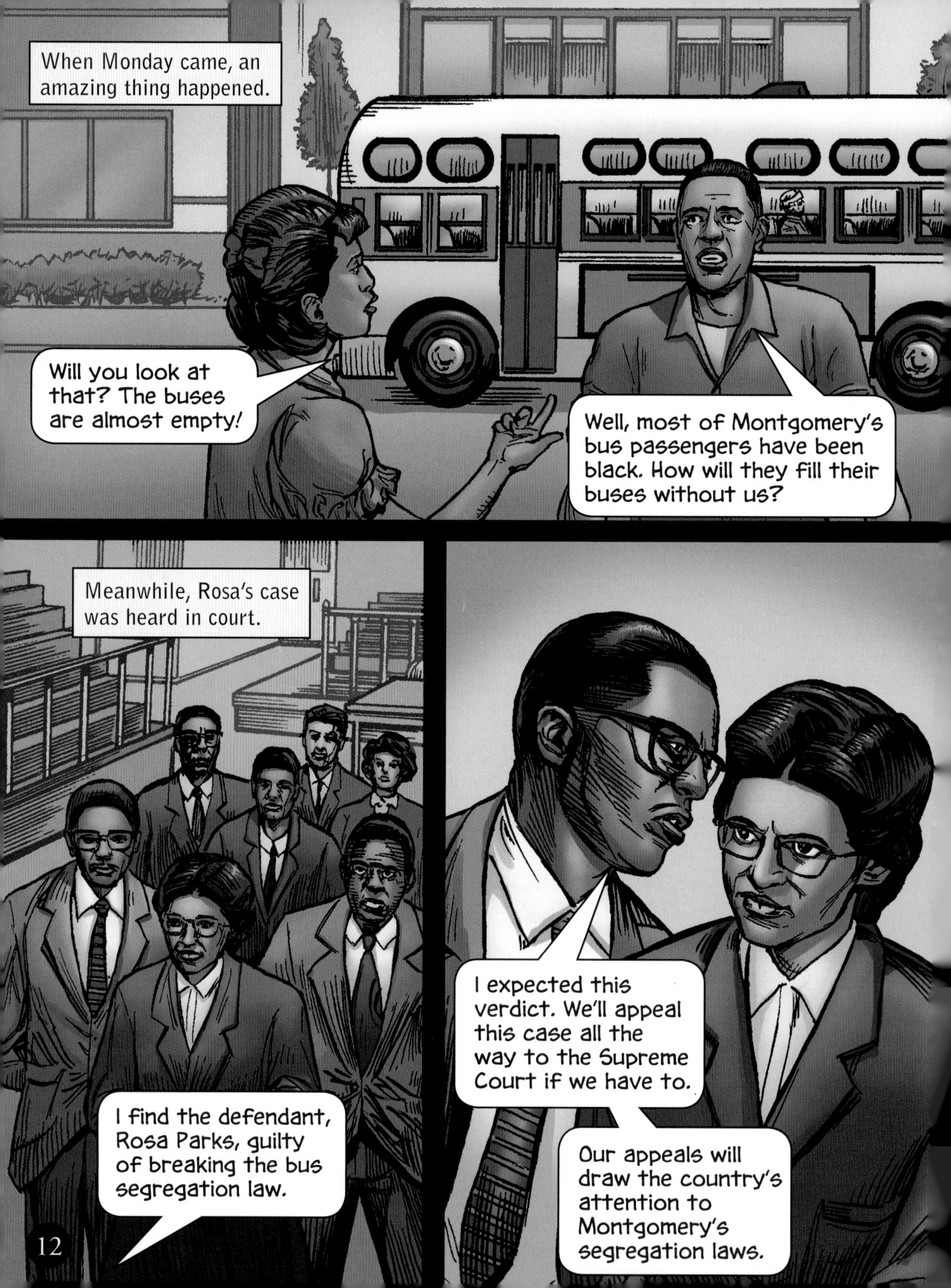

When Monday came, an amazing thing happened.
Will you look at that? The buses are almost empty!
Well, most of Montgomery's bus passengers have been black. How will they fill their buses without us?
Meanwhile, Rosa's case was heard in court.
I find the defendant, Rosa Parks, guilty of breaking the bus segregation law.
I expected this verdict. We'll appeal this case all the way to the Supreme Court if we have to.
Our appeals will draw the country's attention to Montgomery's segregation laws.

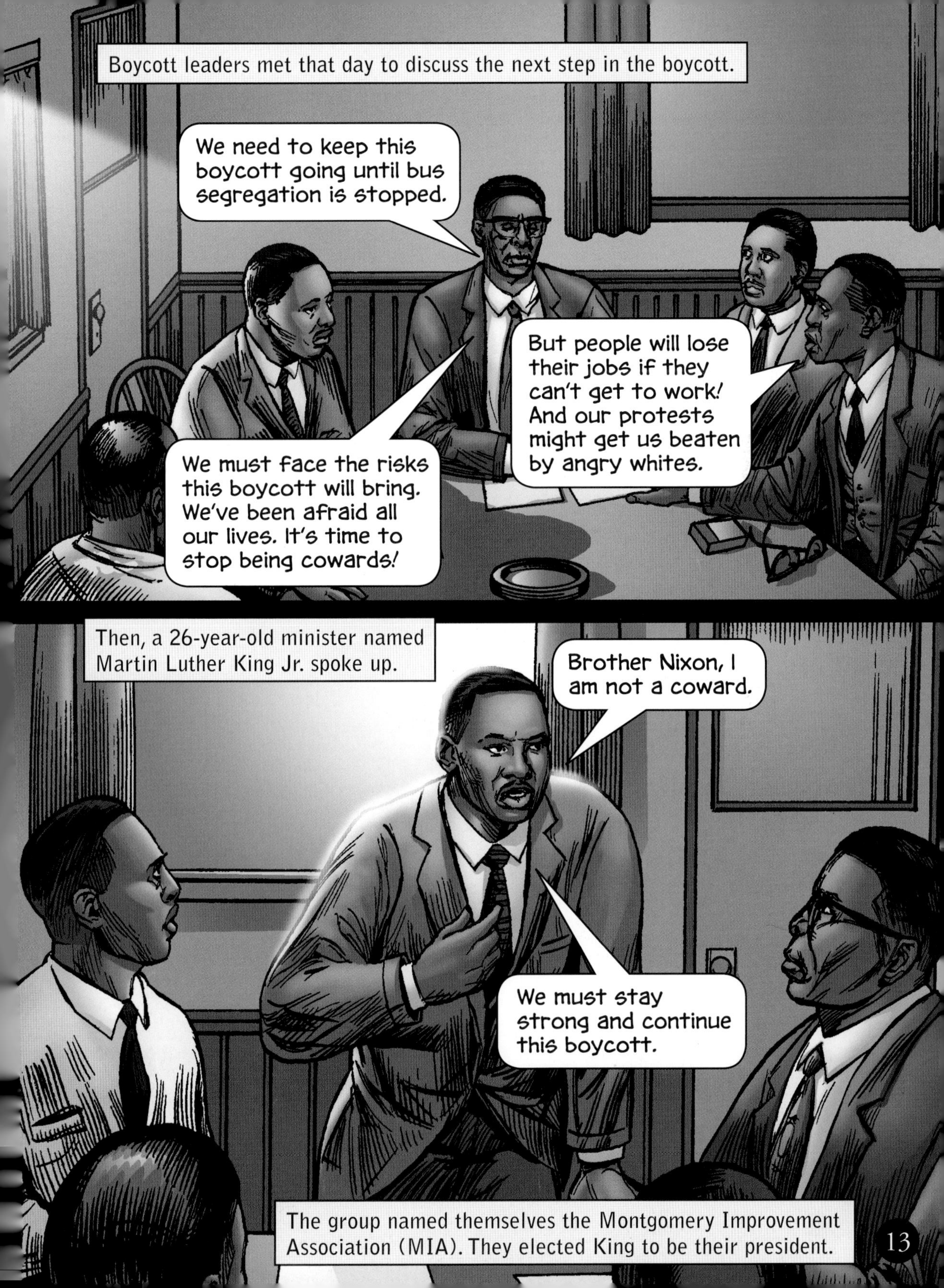
Boycott leaders met that day to discuss the next step in the boycott.
We need to keep this boycott going until bus segregation is stopped.
But people will lose their jobs if they can't get to work! And our protests might get us beaten by angry whites.
We must face the risks this boycott will bring. We've been afraid all our lives. It's time to stop being cowards!
Then, a 26-year-old minister named Martin Luther King Jr. spoke up.
Brother Nixon, I am not a coward.
We must stay strong and continue this boycott.
The group named themselves the Montgomery Improvement Association (MIA). They elected King to be their president.

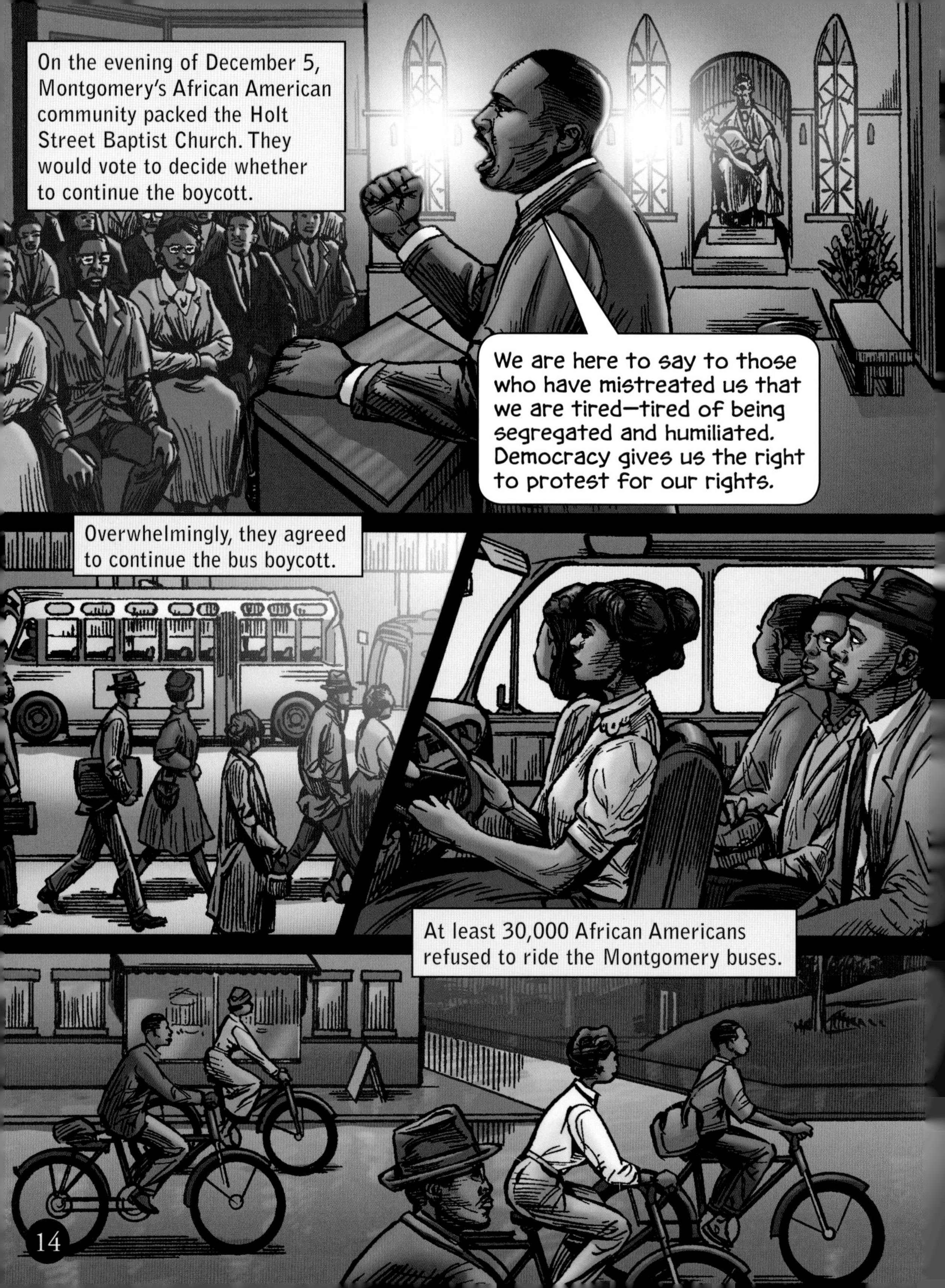
On the evening of December 5, Montgomery's African American community packed the Holt Street Baptist Church. They would vote to decide whether to continue the boycott.
We are here to say to those who have mistreated us that we are tired—tired of being segregated and humiliated. Democracy gives us the right to protest for our rights.
Overwhelmingly, they agreed to continue the bus boycott.
At least 30,000 African Americans refused to ride the Montgomery buses.

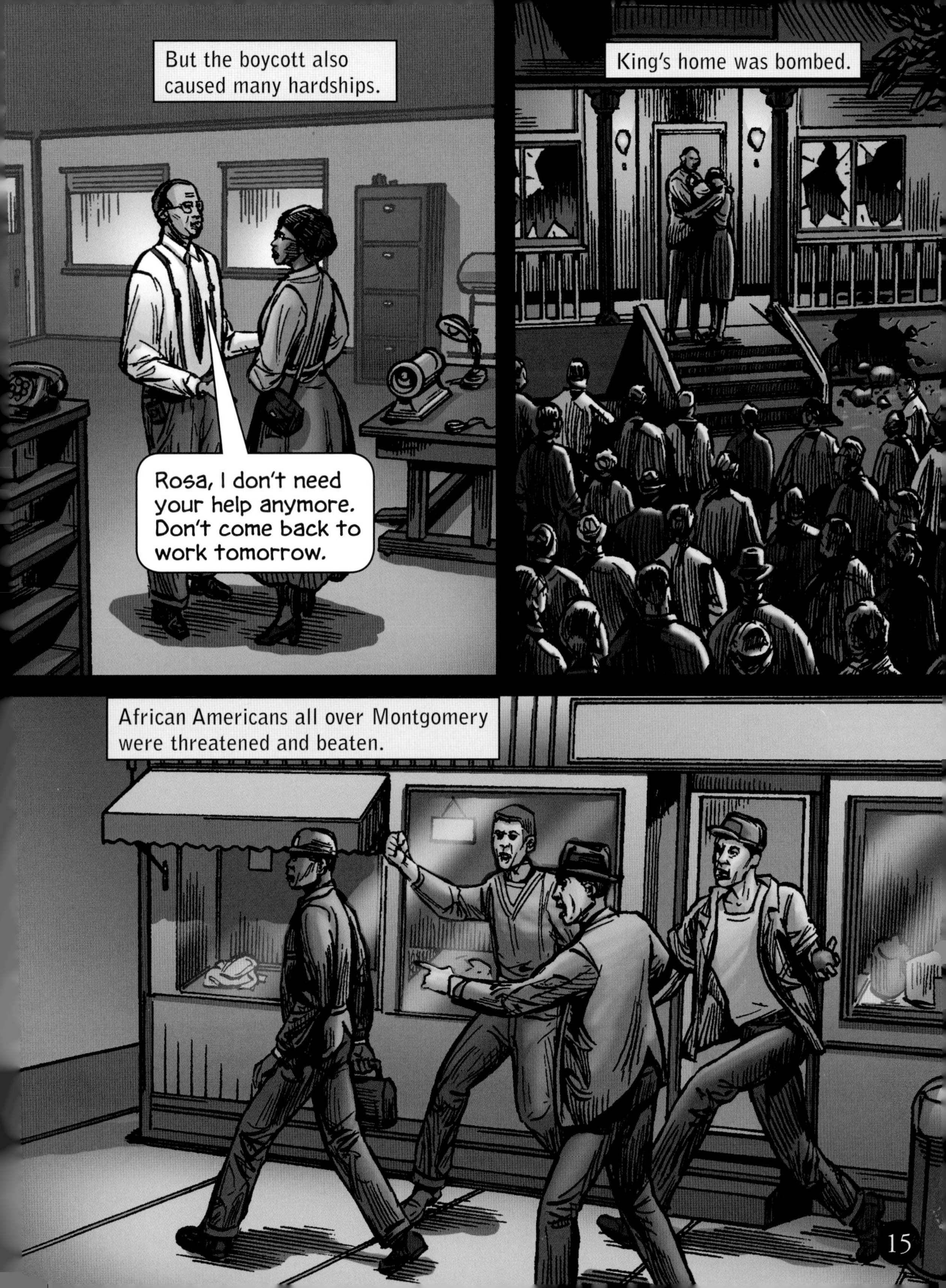
But the boycott also caused many hardships.
Rosa, I don't need your help anymore. Don't come back to work tomorrow.
King's home was bombed.
African Americans all over Montgomery were threatened and beaten.

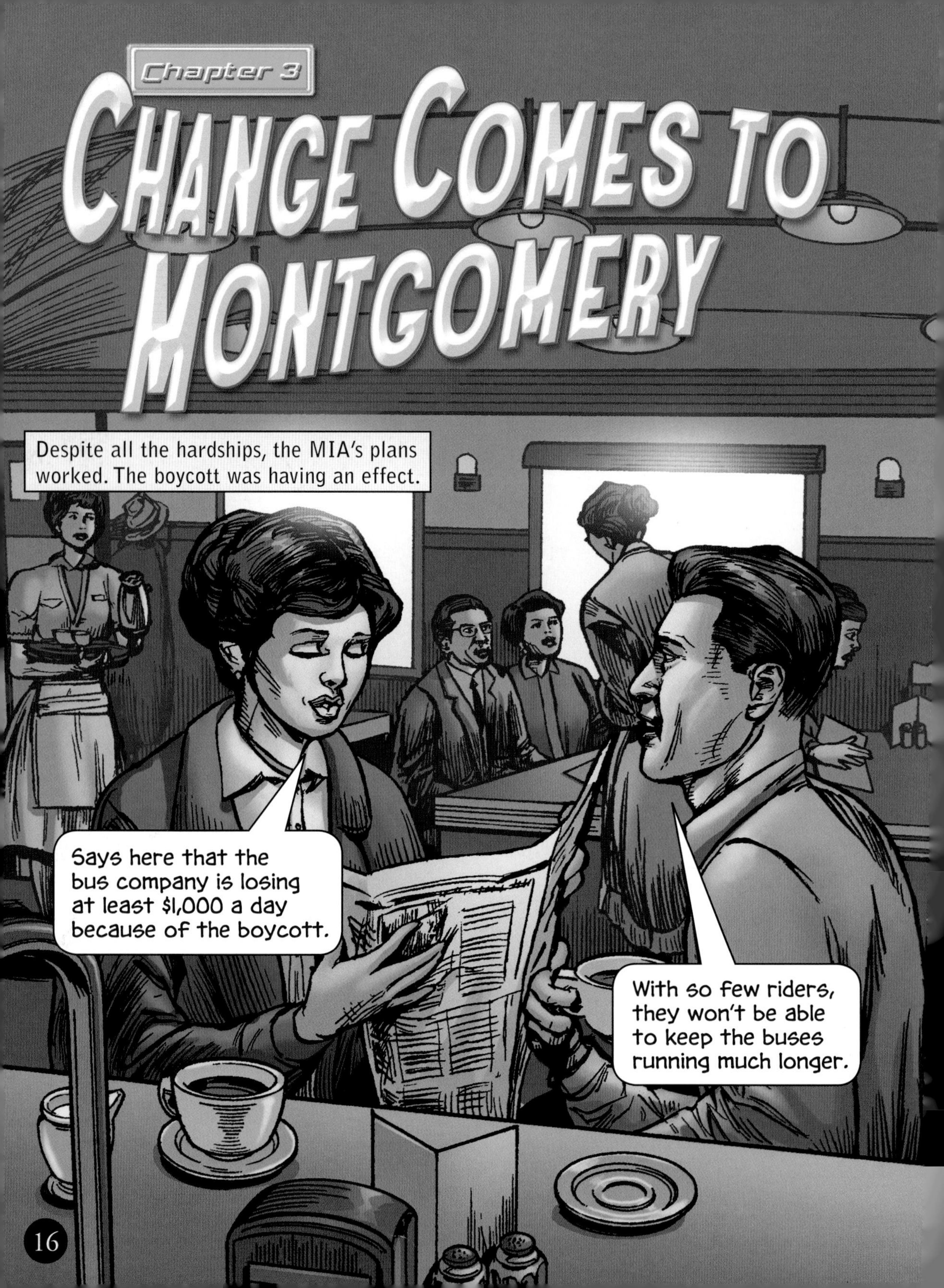
Chapter 3
CHANGE COMES TO MONTGOMERY
Despite all the hardships, the MIA's plans worked. The boycott was having an effect.
Says here that the bus company is losing at least $1,000 a day because of the boycott.
With so few riders, they won't be able to keep the buses running much longer.

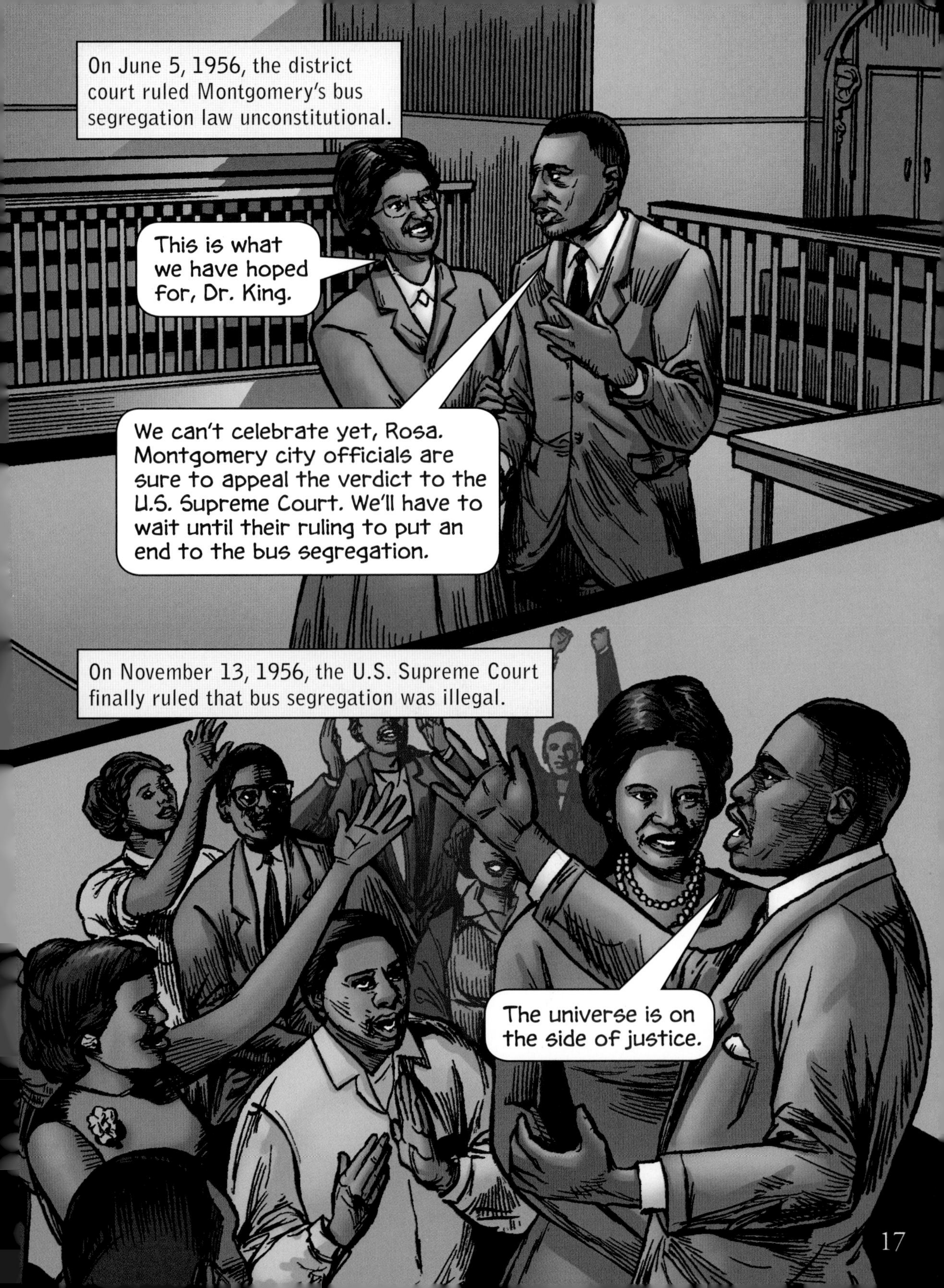
On June 5, 1956, the district court ruled Montgomery's bus segregation law unconstitutional.
This is what we have hoped for, Dr. King.
We can't celebrate yet, Rosa. Montgomery city officials are sure to appeal the verdict to the U.S. Supreme Court. We'll have to wait until their ruling to put an end to the bus segregation.
On November 13, 1956, the U.S. Supreme Court finally ruled that bus segregation was illegal.
The universe is on the side of justice.

One month later, Montgomery buses were no longer segregated. The boycott had lasted 13 months.
Finally, our long wait for equality on public buses has come to an end.

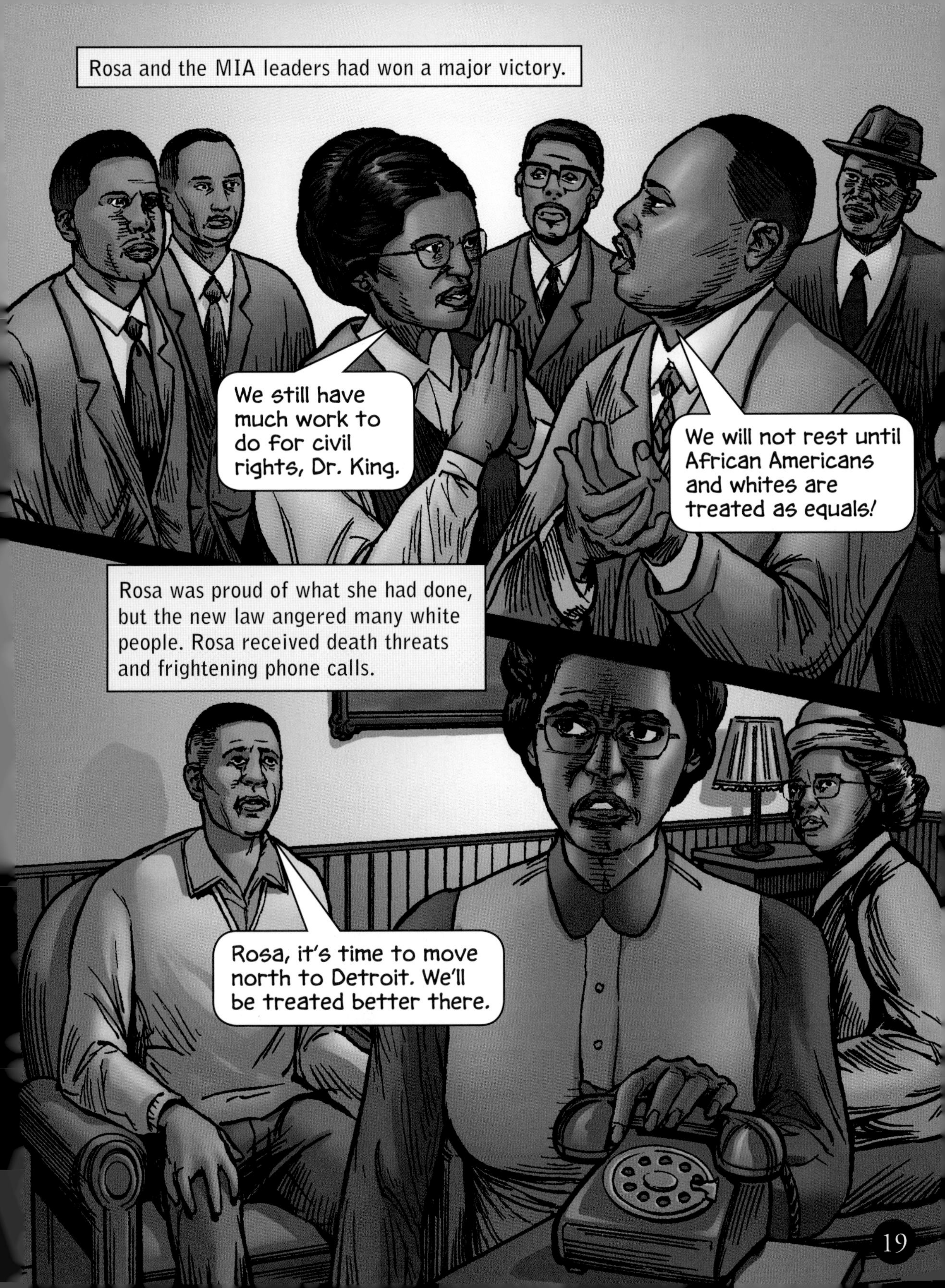
Rosa and the MIA leaders had won a major victory.
We still have much work to do for civil rights, Dr. King.
We will not rest until African Americans and whites are treated as equals!
Rosa was proud of what she had done, but the new law angered many white people. Rosa received death threats and frightening phone calls.
Rosa, it's time to move north to Detroit. We'll be treated better there.

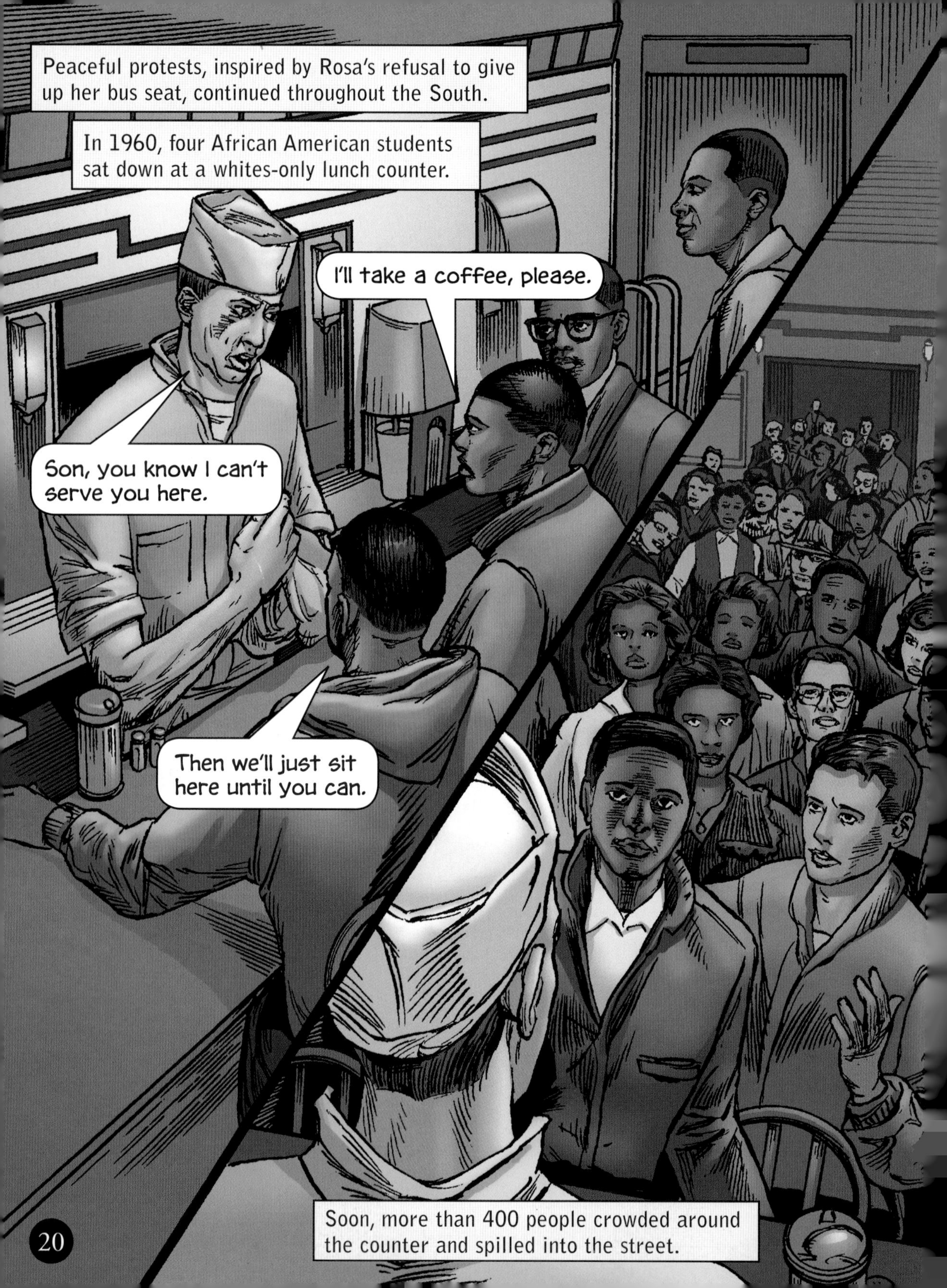

Peaceful protests, inspired by Rosa's refusal to give up her bus seat, continued throughout the South.
In 1960, four African American students sat down at a whites-only lunch counter.
I'll take a coffee, please.
Son, you know I can't serve you here.
Then we'll just sit here until you can.
Soon, more than 400 people crowded around the counter and spilled into the street.

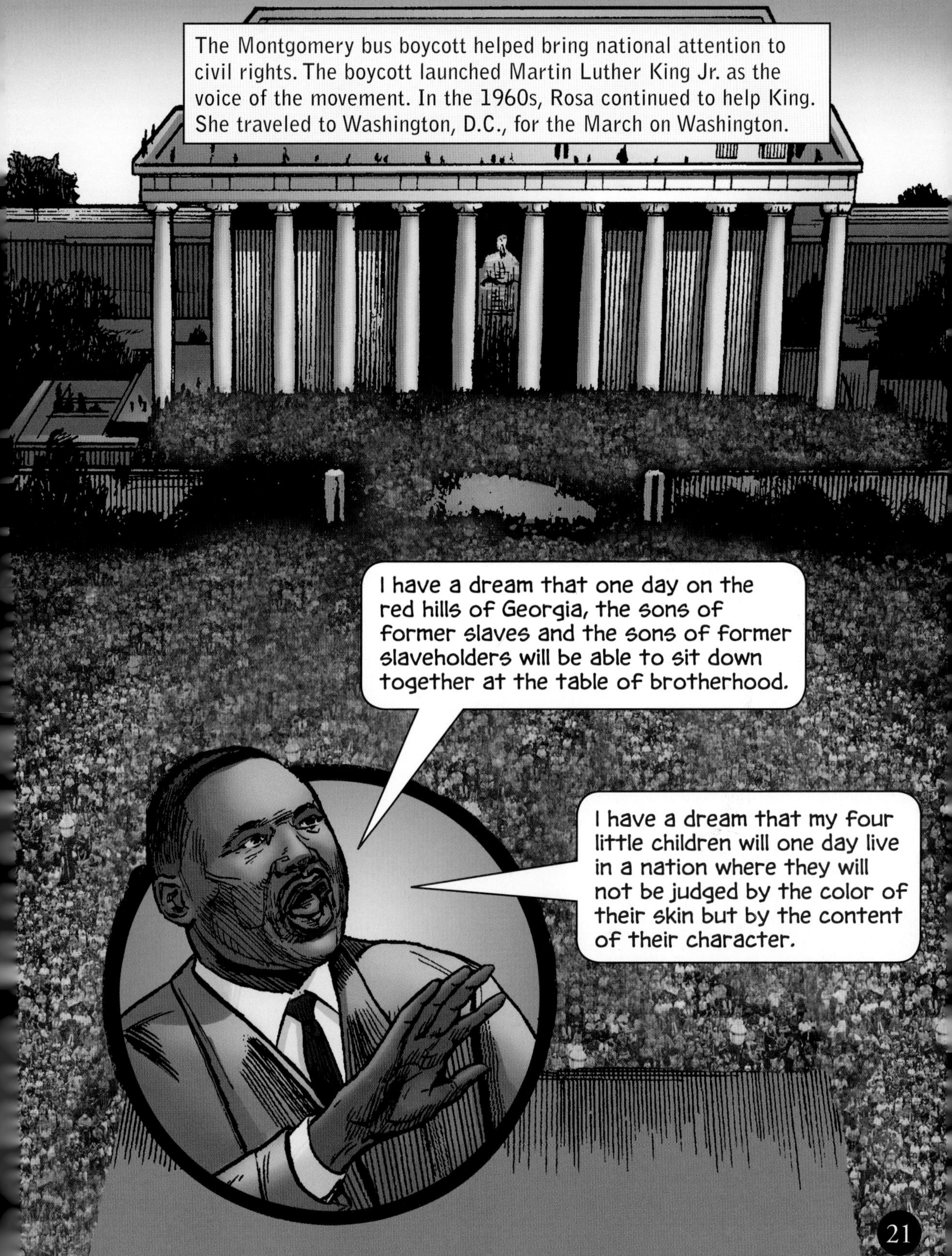
The Montgomery bus boycott helped bring national attention to civil rights. The boycott launched Martin Luther King Jr. as the voice of the movement. In the 1960s, Rosa continued to help King. She traveled to Washington, D.C., for the March on Washington.
I have a dream that one day on the red hills of Georgia, the sons of former slaves and the sons of former slaveholders will be able to sit down together at the table of brotherhood.
I have a dream that my four little children will one day live in a nation where they will not be judged by the color of their skin but by the content of their character.

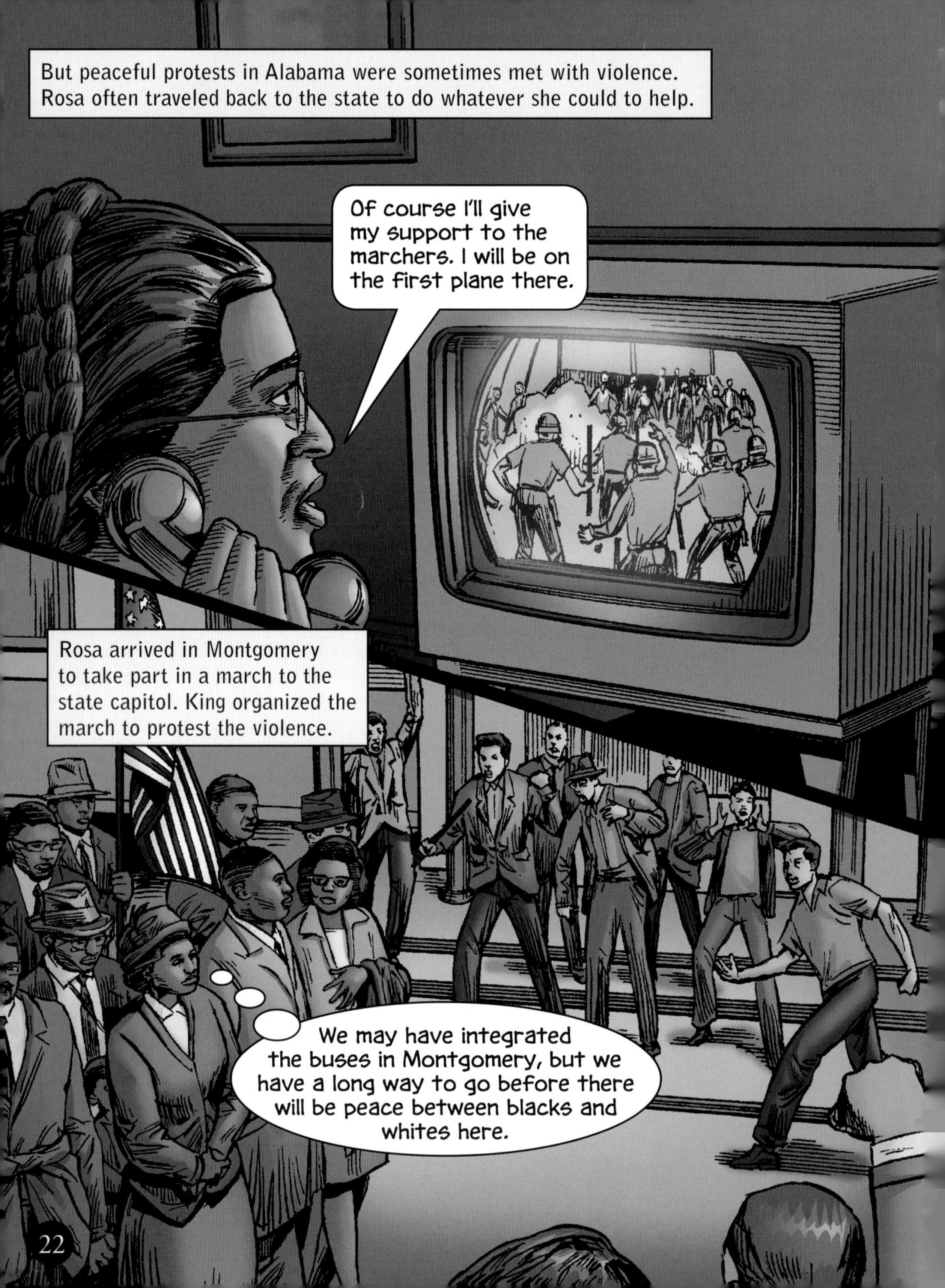
But peaceful protests in Alabama were sometimes met with violence. Rosa often traveled back to the state to do whatever she could to help.
Of course I'll give my support to the marchers. I will be on the first plane there.
Rosa arrived in Montgomery to take part in a march to the state capitol. King organized the march to protest the violence.
We may have integrated the buses in Montgomery, but we have a long way to go before there will be peace between blacks and whites here.

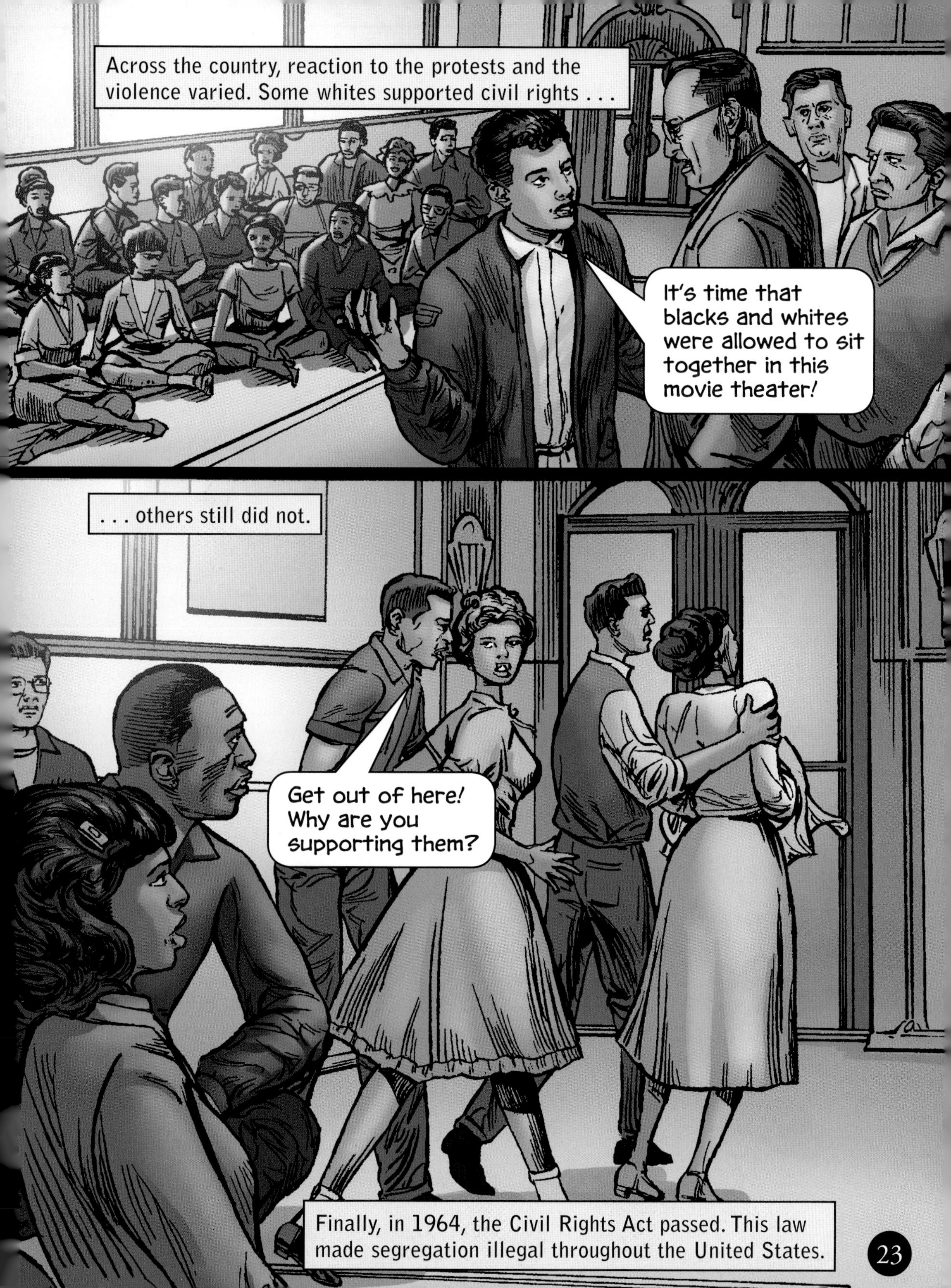
Across the country, reaction to the protests and the violence varied. Some whites supported civil rights . . .
It's time that blacks and whites were allowed to sit together in this movie theater!
. . . others still did not.
Get out of here! Why are you supporting them?
Finally, in 1964, the Civil Rights Act passed. This law made segregation illegal throughout the United States.

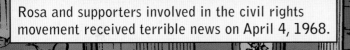

Chapter 4
LEAVING HER MARK

Rosa and supporters involved in the civil rights movement received terrible news on April 4, 1968.

Peaceful protestor Dr. Martin Luther King Jr. has died of a gunshot wound.

Oh, Mother! We have lost our greatest leader. We knew the risks of fighting for equality were great.

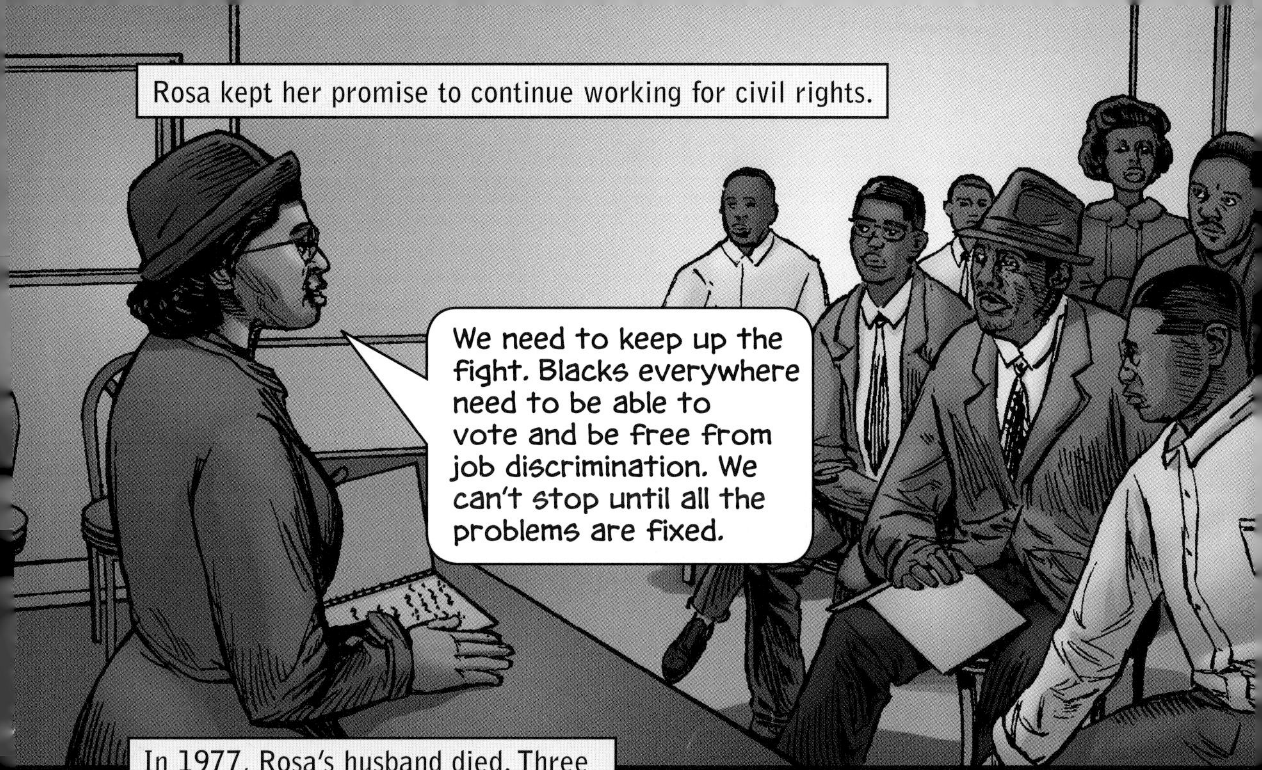
Rosa kept her promise to continue working for civil rights.
We need to keep up the fight. Blacks everywhere need to be able to vote and be free from job discrimination. We can't stop until all the problems are fixed.

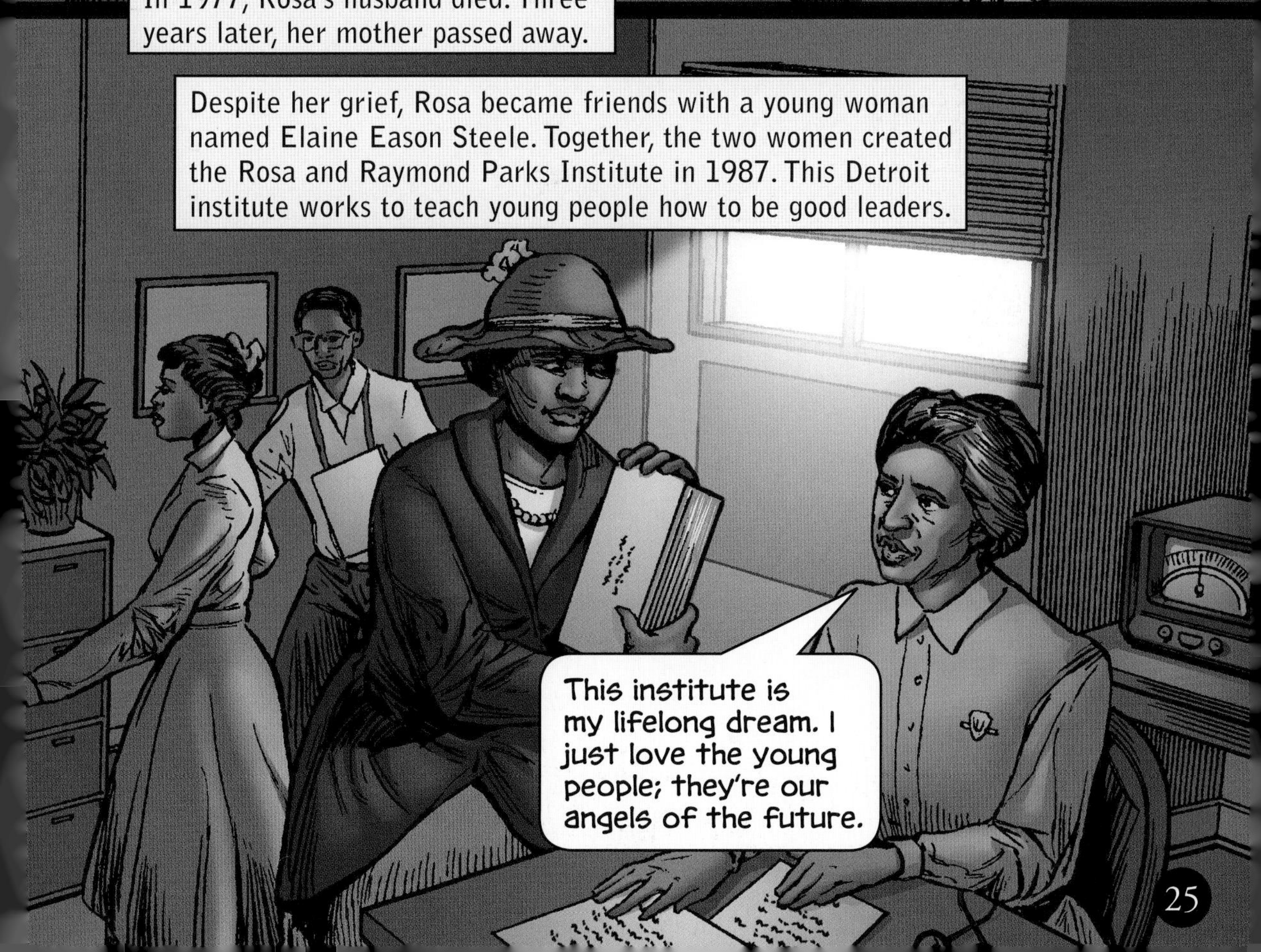
In 1977, Rosa's husband died. Three years later, her mother passed away.
Despite her grief, Rosa became friends with a young woman named Elaine Eason Steele. Together, the two women created the Rosa and Raymond Parks Institute in 1987. This Detroit institute works to teach young people how to be good leaders.
This institute is my lifelong dream. I just love the young people; they're our angels of the future.

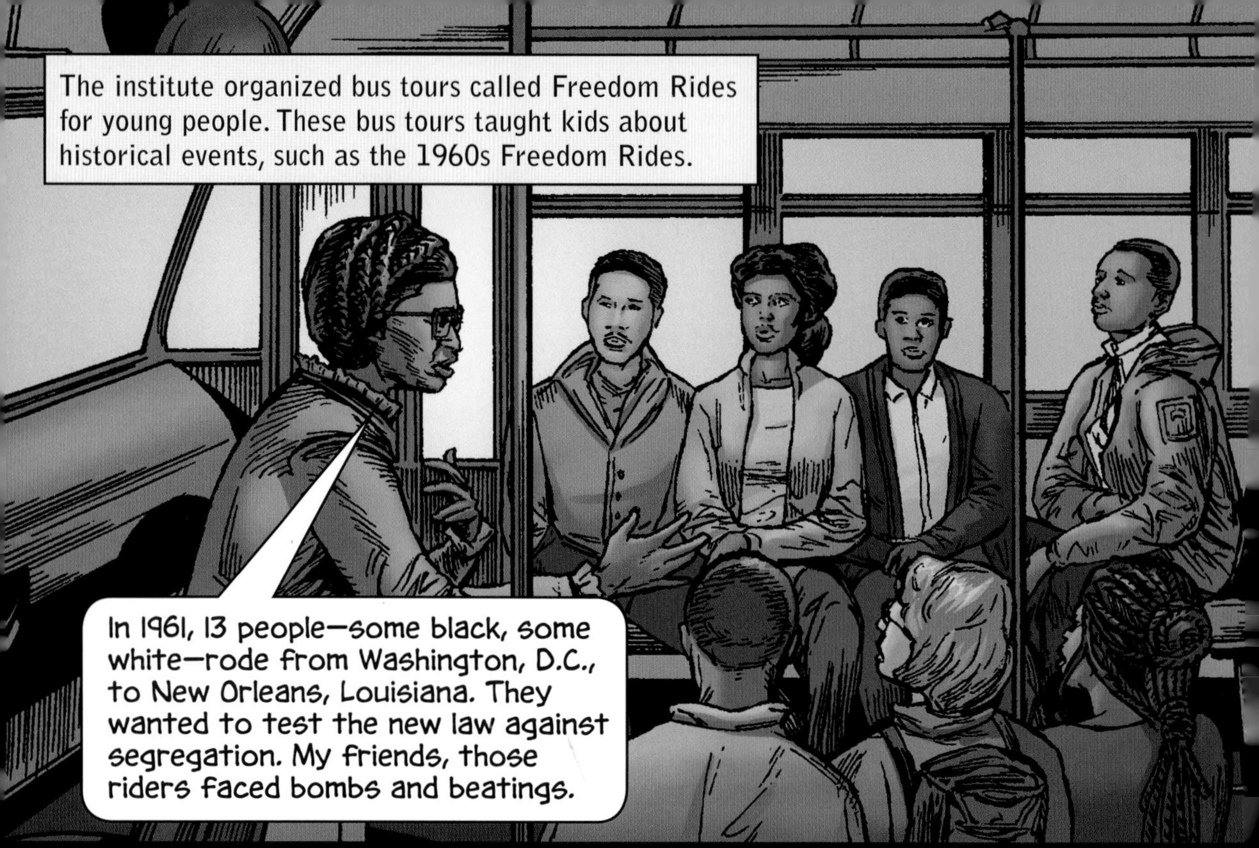
The institute organized bus tours called Freedom Rides for young people. These bus tours taught kids about historical events, such as the 1960s Freedom Rides.
In 1961, 13 people—some black, some white—rode from Washington, D.C., to New Orleans, Louisiana. They wanted to test the new law against segregation. My friends, those riders faced bombs and beatings.

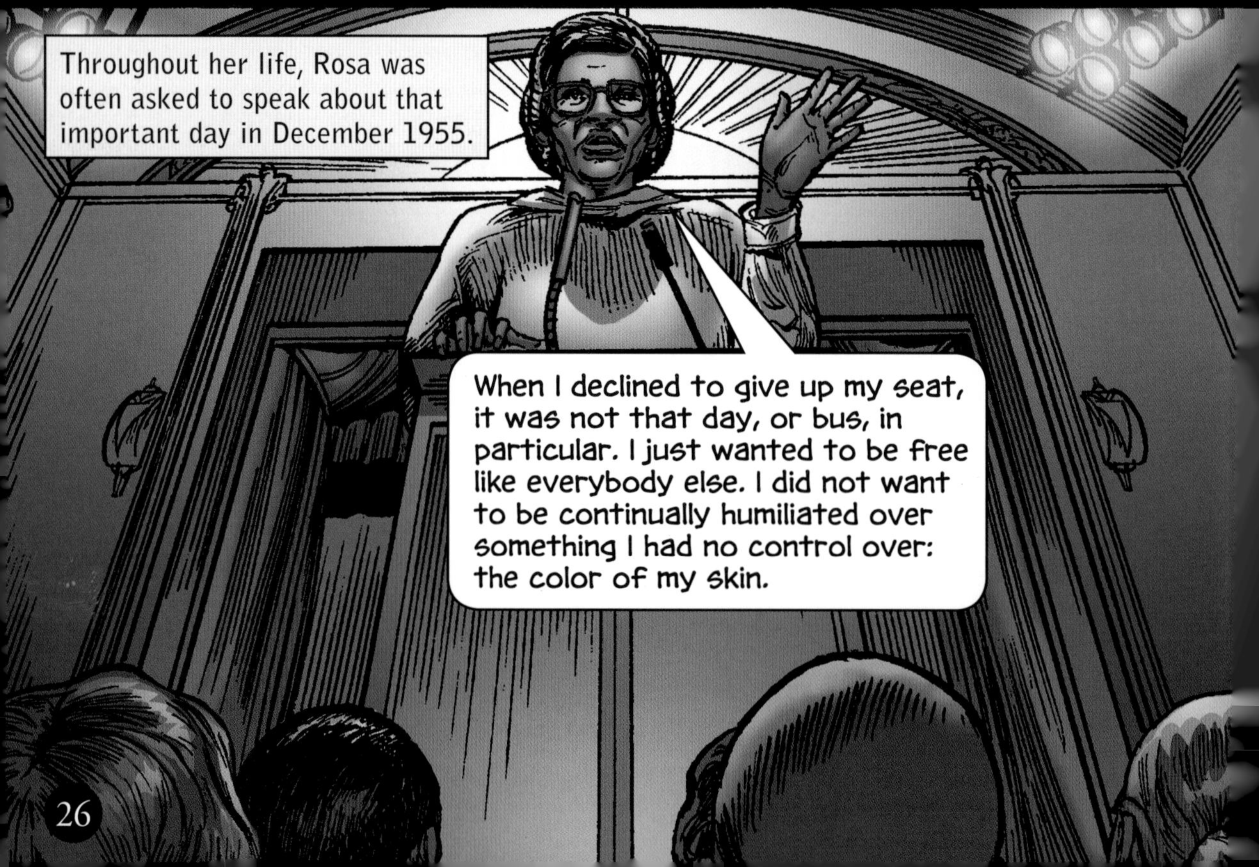
Throughout her life, Rosa was often asked to speak about that important day in December 1955.
When I declined to give up my seat, it was not that day, or bus, in particular. I just wanted to be free like everybody else. I did not want to be continually humiliated over something I had no control over: the color of my skin.

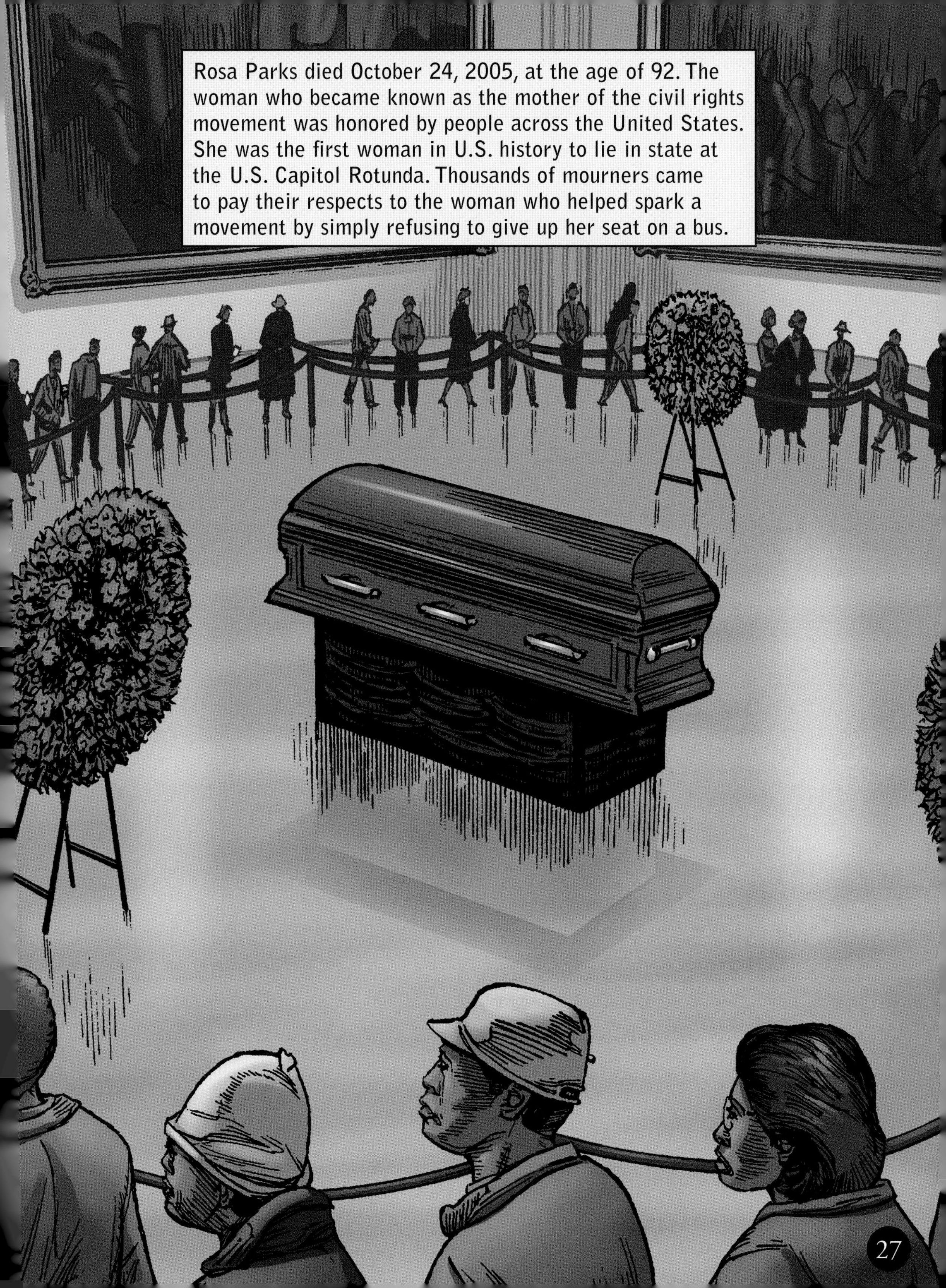
Rosa Parks died October 24, 2005, at the age of 92. The woman who became known as the mother of the civil rights movement was honored by people across the United States. She was the first woman in U.S. history to lie in state at the U.S. Capitol Rotunda. Thousands of mourners came to pay their respects to the woman who helped spark a movement by simply refusing to give up her seat on a bus.

More about

ROSA PARKS

Rosa Parks was born February 4, 1913, in Tuskegee, Alabama. Her parents were James and Leona McCauley.

NAACP stands for the National Association for the Advancement of Colored People. It formed in the early 1900s. Rosa became a member in 1943.

A white supremacy group called the Ku Klux Klan (KKK) terrorized African Americans for many years. The KKK often beat and killed African Americans. When Rosa was young, she sat up late with her grandfather, guarding the house against KKK attacks.

Because she was so kind and gentle, many people thought that Rosa disapproved of using force in the fight for civil rights. In reality, Rosa believed that it was important to stand up for human rights, even if that meant sometimes using force.

- Two women had refused to give up their bus seats before Rosa did in 1955. These women were arrested, just like Rosa. But it was Rosa's character that made her the best person to represent the fight for bus integration.

- In 1956, Rosa posed for a photograph that soon became famous. She boarded a bus and a white reporter posed behind her. For many people, this image symbolized bus integration. The driver that day was the same driver who had her arrested the year before.

- From 1987 to 2000, about 5,000 young people participated in activities at the Rosa and Raymond Parks Institute.

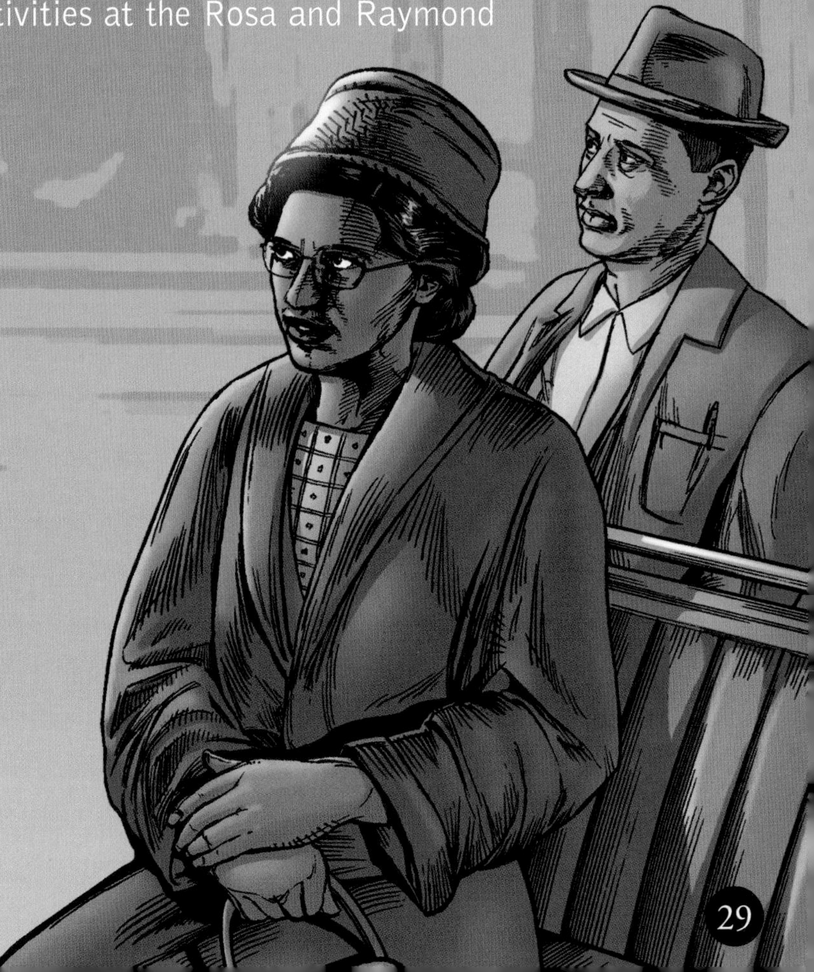

GLOSSARY

appeal (uh-PEEL)—to ask for a decision made by a court of law to be changed

bail (BAYL)—a sum of money paid to a court to allow someone accused of a crime to be set free until his or her trial

boycott (BOI-kot)—to refuse to take part in something as a way of making a protest

integration (in-tuh-GRAY-shuhn)—the act or practice of making facilities open to people of all races and ethnic groups

segregation (seg-ruh-GAY-shuhn)—the act or practice of keeping people or groups apart because of race

verdict (VUR-dikt)—the decision of a jury on whether an accused person is guilty or not guilty

INTERNET SITES

FactHound offers a safe, fun way to find Internet sites related to this book. All of the sites on FactHound have been researched by our staff.

Here's how:
1. Visit *www.facthound.com*
2. Choose your grade level.
3. Type in this book ID **0736864954** for age-appropriate sites. You may also browse subjects by clicking on letters, or by clicking on pictures and words.
4. Click on the **Fetch It** button.

FactHound will fetch the best sites for you!

READ MORE

Edwards, Pamela Duncan. *The Bus Ride That Changed History: The Story of Rosa Parks.* Boston: Houghton Mifflin, 2005.

Miller, Jake. *The Montgomery Bus Boycott: Integrating Public Buses.* Library of the Civil Rights Movement. New York: Rosen, 2004.

Ritchie, Nigel. *The Civil Rights Movement.* Lives in Crisis. Hauppauge, N.Y.: Barron's, 2003.

Steele, Philip. *Rosa Parks and Her Protest for Civil Rights.* Dates with History. North Mankato, Minn.: Smart Apple Media, 2003.

BIBLIOGRAPHY

Brinkley, Douglas. *Rosa Parks.* Penguin Lives Series. New York: Viking, 2000.

Burns, Stewart, ed. *Daybreak of Freedom: The Montgomery Bus Boycott.* Chapel Hill, N.C.: The University of North Carolina Press, 1997.

Parks, Rosa, with Jim Haskins. *My Story.* New York: Dial Books, 1992.

Robinson, Jo Ann Gibson. *The Montgomery Bus Boycott and the Women Who Started It: The Memoir of Jo Ann Gibson Robinson.* Knoxville, Tenn.: University of Tennessee Press, 1987.

INDEX